Blush

Cici. B

♥

For all of the women who have ever had a
hard time moving on after a heartbreak...

You deserve to take back control of your life
and to do the things that make you happy.
You deserve to fall in love with yourself again.
You deserve to fall in love with your life
again.
You deserve to smile, to laugh, and to just be
free.

You deserve,
      to Blush.

           Cici.B

I

Me First This Time

"Bitch you're glowing." My girl Jazzy said as I eased into the booth of the busy restaurant/lounge. "You're late, and you're glowing which only means one thing—you got some D!" She and Angel high fived each other while I rolled my eyes and laughed. "Y'all are a trip and a fuckin half. NO, I did not get any D. My vagina still has them cobwebs on her fuck y'all very much."

The waitress came over and I ordered a Southern and 7 on the rocks. "Wait. Where's Erika?" I asked noticing that one of us was missing. "She couldn't get off work." Jazzy said. Angel batted her eyelashes at me. "Soooo, if you're not getting any D… what's with the glow then?" I looked at her and then at Jazzy. "Damn. A girl can't be in a good mood without it involving sex?" My girls looked at each other —"Hell nah!"

They said in unison and fell out laughing as they high fived again. "Y'all stupid" I told them.

The waitress came back with my drink and I sipped it and smiled. "Nah, you wanna know what it is?" I started. "To be honest I think there comes a point in every woman's life when she realizes that it's gonna be okay... *she's* gonna be okay.

A time when she stops putting other people before herself and starts feeling good about putting herself all the way first. A time when she not only stops going hard for the people who don't go hard for her, but closes the door to them all together and for good. A time when she's ready to take back control of her life and do right by her for a change —and that's where I am right now. I'm in that time zone and I'm feeling hella good about doing right by me." I took another sip of my drink. "Feel me?"

Angel started applauding while Jazzy raised her Lychee martini. "I mean, if that doesn't deserve a toast then I don't know what does!" I beamed from ear to ear and raised my drink too. "Wait!" Angel yelled. "So does this mean you're *not* trying to get any D or a new man anytime soon?" Jazzy and I looked at Angel and shook our heads. "What?!" she asked. "I'm just asking. Shit. Sometimes a girl needs an extra, *extra* glow." She winked. "Do you *feel* me?"

"Anywaaaysss" Jazzy said cutting her eye at Angel and raising her glass towards me again. "Cheers you goddess. After everything you've been through, you deserve this feeling and your rosy ass cheeks. So glow on girl. We love you." I nodded my head in agreement as we all touched glasses. "Thank you boo's. I love y'all right back."

As I sat there with my girls, and my glow, I couldn't help but take a moment to silently say a little prayer and thank God for this new found feeling that I had. Being sad, miserable, heartbroken and stressed out all of the time, and for as long as I had been over a man, I had forgotten what it was like to just be carefree and do the simplest of things—like meeting up with my girls for some drinks and some food—without feeling like I wanted to cry my fucking eyes out every twelve minutes because of an angry argumentative text coming through my phone to fuck up my whole night.

It was the first time in my life that I felt completely empowered, free, and head over heels in love with myself, and wanted to wear the key to my heart around my own neck for a while.

Not to say that I would never give it to anyone ever again—no—because I was still the romantic girl that I always had been, and definitely still believed in great love between two people, but I was no longer willing to compromise myself for it, or to be with or around anyone who didn't want to love me as much as I loved myself. So I wouldn't be handing over that key so easily the next time around. Besides, my mind wasn't focused on falling in love with a man.

My mind was focused on *enjoying* my life.

Was I was swearing off all men? No, not at all.

Men are a part of life. But falling in love with *any* man just wasn't at the top of my list of needs, or wants for that matter—I wanted to be my own woman, for myself. Addressed and known by MY name, instead of being the "girlfriend of" whoever.

I had spent most of my twenties in back to back relationships and because of that, I missed out on a lot of myself and on creating the woman that I wanted to be, because I was so busy being the woman that someone else wanted me to be. I compromised a lot, too much, and when I looked back—that was my very first mistake.

I always let the men that I was with get away with the small things, knowing that I shouldn't have, but not wanting to say anything for fear of starting an argument. But it was those same small things that became redundant, then painful, and then damaging.

Had I put my foot down and stood up for myself sooner, and showed them that I wouldn't be tolerating even the smallest amount of shit... then none of the shit that I went through would have happened. I was the one who taught them how to treat me by keeping my mouth shut all of the time. Letting them get away with the small things.

So at this point, it was just a matter of understanding and accepting that I needed some time to detox.

I felt like there were still parts of me that didn't even really belong to me at all, as they were created just to please someone else, and I knew that it was going to take time to figure out which parts were which and to get entirely rid of the ones that just didn't belong...

But I was cool with that.

For the first time in my life, I was cool with letting
time just do its thing.
I thought back to a conversation I had with my mother
while I was over at her place for dinner a couple of
months earlier. After all the shit I had been through
with my ex, and the toll that she knew it had taken on
me, she just wanted to make sure that I was good.

"So what are you gonna do?" She asked me while we sat
with our coffees digesting our food.

I shrugged my shoulders and smiled. "Whatever feels
good." I answered. "Whatever feels good to me and is
not hurting anyone that I love around me—I'm gonna
do. I've spent so much time NOT feeling good because
of these messy situations that I was being loyal to,
hoping that they'd turn around for the better, and I
just feel like... no. I'm not doing that shit anymore.

I want good vibes. I wanna blush. I wanna smile till my
cheeks hurt. I wanna go on fun dates and then call my
girls in the morning and spill the tea while we laugh. I
wanna hold someone's hand who wants to hold mine,
while we walk and talk about everything or nothing. I
wanna travel with my girls and live in the moment with

them while we create memories that will last a lifetime—and I'm gonna do that. I'm gonna do all of the things that make ME feel good for a change."

She stayed quiet for a moment as she smiled at me, and it was almost like I could see her whole heart in her eyes. "What?" I asked her laughing. "Why are you looking at me like that?" She shook her head. "I'm just really proud of you babygirl. Really, really proud of you."

Thinking about that conversation warmed my soul...

I was proud of me too.

"What's a pretty girl like you doing without a man?"

Getting my shit together—that's what.

♥

2

Fuck It

"So, let him take you out." Angel said through my phone.

I was rushing around my house trying to get my damn life together so I could go run my errands, and was holding the phone to my ear with my shoulder while putting on my mascara in the mirror—because as usual, I couldn't find my stupid earphones and my speakerphone option was acting up. I had met a guy very randomly the week before and was filling her in on the details.

She and the rest of my girls had been on my back about *"meeting new people"* and *"giving someone a chance"* blah blah fucking blah—annoying the entire shit out of me for a while. But truth be told, I had definitely been avoiding the whole putting myself out there thing. So when this cutie with a smooth voice, and a dope vibe approached me out of nowhere and asked for my number (which I never give to anyone) ... I thought to myself *fuck it. Maybe it'll do me some good to talk to someone new. Shit, I am single after all.*

So I gave it to him.

We had been texting/talking back and forth for about week and honestly he was cool for the most part but there were a couple of things that were making me a little uneasy. During our first hour long phone call, while we were going back and forth exchanging info about all of the basics—favorite color, favorite movies, favorite foods—and all that shit, he let me know that he had a child.

Now for me that was strike one. I had already just been through this baby mother shit with my ex and I wasn't trying to go through it again.

Like, ever.

So as soon as he said that my mind sprung right into "abort mission" mode, but at the very same time I could just *hear* every single one of my girlfriends voices in my head yelling at once— *"learn to give dudes a chaaaance, stop being so picky, you just never knooooow until you trryyyyy."*

So... I bit my tongue and decided to listen to my friends in my head.

The conversation continued just fine and now we were at the part where we were telling each other which areas of town we lived in. I told him mine, and included that I lived alone, and then he told me his and told me he lived with his mom.

Okay... *strike fucking two much?*

"Is your mom sick or something?" I asked.
I just wanted to know why the fuck a thirty year old grown ass man was still living with his mom, and the only thing that I could think of asking him without sounding like a rude ass bitch, was if she was sick. Because if she *was* then that would make perfect sense—right?

"Nah she's not sick or anything like that." he answered with a light chuckle. "I just don't see why I would pay rent anywhere, when I'm perfectly comfortable here and don't have to pay for anything."

...great. he's a cheapskate.

On the one hand I could see how that made sense. Why have a bunch of bills for no reason when you don't have to? But on the other hand...*uuummm*, you're a grown ass man. Don't you want your own space? What do you do? Sneak girls in and out of your bedroom in your mommy's house? Put your hand over a girl's mouth while you're having sex so your mommy doesn't hear? Do you bring girls over to "chill" in your room like it's fucking highschool all over again? Bruh... come *on*.

The more I thought about it, the more I just wasn't feeling it but once *again* my friends in my head came through and once *again*, I bit my tongue and continued the conversation without a hiccup like it was still *aalll* good.

After a week of texting back and forth just shooting the shit, I got a morning text from him asking to take me out for dinner anywhere I wanted that night. As much I was trying to be open minded, the two strikes still just weren't sitting right with me, so I simply responded that I would have to check my schedule and get back to him.

After explaining all of this to my girl, "so, let him take you out" was her dumb ass nonchalant response.

I closed the tube of mascara, set it down on the counter and lifted the phone with my hand off of my shoulder.

"So that's it? All you're going to say is 'let him take you out?' Angel you're always so damn eager to get me to go on a date with somebody, were you even listening to me? Did you miss the part about him having a kid AND living at his damn momma's house or are you just going to skip right over that like I never said it?" She started laughing—"Well! So what if he has a kid B, and so what he lives with his mom? I'm not telling you to marry the guy. I didn't say go fall in love with him. I didn't even say have sex with him! All I'm saying is to let him take you out. Shit, you haven't let a man take you out in FOREVER. All you do is work and go home, work and go home. You've turned into such a bore. Where's the B we know huh?! Where's the out and about, living life B that we know? Girl, I'm just sayin... let a man wine and dine you! And shit, maybe he'll do excellent on the wine part and then you can be open to getting some dick too! *Now* I'm sayin' it. 'Cause come to think of it Lord KNOWS you *do* need some new fucking dick. Okay?"

I had left my bathroom and was now in my shoe closet pulling out my nude pumps.

"I hate you and you make me sick Angel. I just want you to know that." I told her. "I love you too boo!" she said back to me through more laughter. I smiled, shook my head and sighed. "Anyways, I'll think about it while I'm on the road. I'm late as shit."—"Girl what else is new? You're always late as shit." I took my phone off of my ear and held it up to my face, "BYE ANGEL." I smiled and hit the end button.

I shoved it into the back pocket of my dark blue skinny jeans, grabbed my soft cream colored blazer off of the chair beside me and put it on over my white loose fitting t-shirt. I gave myself one last look over in the full mirror and gave my long jet black hair one last brush through as I thought about what Angel had said.

Fuck it.

I pulled my phone back out and sent my two striker a text—"I'm free for dinner tonight... and I could go for some awesome wings. 8pm works for me."
I grabbed my car keys, my bag, threw on my shades and headed out the door as I sang *"que sera, sera... whatever will be, will be..."*

Sometimes in life, you've just gotta go with the flow and trust that it will lead you exactly where you're supposed to be, or to a lesson that was meant for you to learn.

♥

3

Lesson Learned

We met at the restaurant.

I pulled up first and waited for him by the entrance and he pulled up about 5 minutes later. We greeted with a hug and he immediately complimented me on my attire. The restaurant I had chosen wasn't anything fancy shmancy (I'm not a complicated girl, I just wanted some damn wings) so I was dressed casually in some black jeans, a white sweater with black lace up combat boots and my red and white varsity jacket.

I smiled and thanked him. "You ain't looking too shabby yourself, Sir." I said. He too was dressed casually in a gray polo sweater with dark blue jeans and some Tim's. He looked nice—smooth.
He opened the door of the restaurant and gestured with his hand, "after you Madame."
You damn straight after me I thought to myself walking in. After the hostess showed us to our table and we

were settled in and ordered our food, we got to chitchatting.

While he talked I stared at him and went over the details of his face. He had soft looking mocha skin, with barely any hair on his face and deep brown eyes. I could tell by the evenness of his hairline and his low fade, that he had just gotten a fresh cut that day. He was definitely a cutie—not over the top smack you in the face with gorgeousness mind you—but, he was a cutie. I moved my eyes down to his hands and immediately took noticed of his clean fingernails. I mentally nodded in approval.

Clean fingernails = frequent hand washer.

As he spoke, my mind wandered off and I tried to imagine what he would be like in bed. I tried to picture myself lying on my back while lifting my head up just a tad to watch him work his tongue in between my legs. But the thought of it did nothing for me. I wasn't even *slightly* aroused. Matter of fact, there was zero sexual chemistry between us. Well, maybe *he* could have been sexually attracted to me, but the feeling wasn't mutual. Still listening to him talk (kind of) I quickly realized that it was because he hadn't really done anything to seduce my mind; and I needed that to be turned on. I

needed to be intrigued. I needed to drown in curiosity.
I needed that spark. That flame.

That... something special.

But that something special just wasn't him.
So right there I drew the conclusion that if anything
we'd just be cool, but nothing more. Yes, unbeknownst
to him I had "friendzoned" his ass. It's true what they
say you know—we women know within the first
couple of minutes of being around a man whether
we're going to have sex with him, or not.

Our drinks came first. He had ordered a beer
(Heineken) while I had ordered a strawberry daiquiri
with an extra shot of rum. *Fuck it.* It was my day off
and it had been a long ass week and gawt damn it, I
needed that extra shot.

The night was running perfectly fine as we talked
about regular things and laughed about the small
things that we did have in common, and when the food
came, I stuffed my fucking face. I'm not the kind of girl
who's shy to eat in front of guys. There's food. We
came to eat. Best believe I'm fucking EATING.

After we were done, naturally, the bill came and he picked it up off the table to examine it.

"Wow." He said as his eyebrows raised.
"A hundred and eighty dollars?!"

I looked at him confused. "Huh?" The girls and I went to that joint all the time and that's usually what the bill looked like for the four of us without drinks, so I couldn't understand why the bill would be that much for just two of us.

"Lemme see that." I said reaching over the table grabbing the paper out of his hands. I quickly scanned the bottom of it—78.64$—I looked up at him. "Just kidding," he said through a grin and a chuckle. "You should have seen your face. Looked like you were ready to curse everyone in this place!" I laughed too. Because you can bet your ass that I ready to flag down that waitress and give her a couple of good cuss words.

"Ha ha ha. Very funny." I gave him back the bill and and took a sip of my drink. He took the paper back in his hand and went over it—again.

I don't know why, but my silent alarm went off in my gut. 'Everything okay?' I asked him. He moved his eyes

off of the paper and onto me. "Yea, nah everything's alright. It's still kind of pricey though, I'm just going over the individual prices." I laughed because he was obviously joking again. *Right?*
"Sure it is." I said getting up from the table. "I'm going to wash my hands I'll be right back."

Now normally in life when a woman gets up to go to the bathroom, by the time she returns, the bill is paid and it's time to go. But apparently *my* life still wasn't quite at level normal as yet, because when I got back to the table the bill was still in his hands—unpaid.

"The waitress still didn't come for that yet?" I asked casually as I slid back into the booth looking around for her. "Nah she didn't come yet. I'm just still amazed that the bill is like 80 bucks."
Okay. He wasn't joking this time. As I stared at him I realized he was dead ass serious and this eighty fucking dollar bill was hurting his feelings. "Awww, do you want to split the bill?" I asked obviously just kidding. "Sure!" He answered looking up at me, relieved. "If you don't mind, that would be great."

Now hold on just a gawt damn fucking minute.........

If I was trying to find a spark from him earlier, well now my whole body was on fucking fire. Was I really on a FIRST date with a man who was about to have NO PROBLEM SPLITTING A MEASLY EIGHTY DOLLAR FUCKING DINNER BILL? I shot the rest of my drink in his face and stormed the fuck out of there...

In my mind though.

In my mind, is where I shot the rest of my drink in his face. In fucking reality, I forced a nice smile and opened my wallet, pulled out a crisp fifty dollar bill and placed it on the table.

Just relax and stay calm B. You're a lady and you're going to stay calm.

As I got up from the table to put my jacket on, he reached into his pocket and pulled out TEN DOLLARS IN COINS—loonies and fucking toonies—to give me my 'change'.

"Here" he said, holding the CHANGE in his hand out towards me.

At that point I began looking around for Jazzy, Angel, and Erika because I was SURE that this whole thing was just a really funny joke that they had set up, and that they were somewhere in this restaurant with their phones out making a hilarious video to put on YouTube titled—"Hilarious Friend Pranks."

But no... my girlfriends were nowhere in sight. It was just him. Holding out his stupid ass change, in his stupid ass hand, insisting that I take it. God it took everything in me to keep that fucking fake smile on my lips, but I kept it and shook my head. "No booboo, that's quite alright. I don't need change." I finished putting on my jacket, grabbed my keys and wallet off the table and turned to walk away. "No but we're splitting the bill. So this is your half babe."

Babe?

I stopped, my back towards him. *Just keep smiling B. It's almost over. You're doing good. Just keep smiling.*

As I turned to face him, the waitress had come to collect. "All set here?" She asked in a bubbly happy-go-lucky tone. "Yes." I responded. "Sweetie" I said to him, "leave all the change on the table for the waitress." He did so silently along with HIS HALF of

the bill, then followed me out of the restaurant and
walked me to my car.

What a fucking gentlemanly thing of him to do.

"So, what do you want to do now?" he asked leaning in
closer to me.

*What do I want do now? Should we go for Ice Cream
somewhere and SPLIT that bill too you dipshit?!*

You know, there are women in this world who don't
mind being asked out on a date, and then splitting the
bill—and that's cool—but I wasn't that girl. To each is
their own but I still believed in some good old
fashioned courtship *especially* on FIRST dates.

Like come on.

I really wanted to give him a light cursing, because I
was so annoyed, but there was no point. Clearly he and
I lived in two different worlds and in his world, an
eighty dollar bill was simply unheard of and asking his
date to *split* the bill was perfectly normal. Deep down I
knew this shit was my fault anyways. I'd gone on a date
with a man—against my better judgment—all because

I let my wonderful friends—who meant
well—influence my brain. So you know what?

Lesson learned. The end.

"Actually, I'm really full and a little light headed from
my drinks so I think I'm going to call it a night, go
home and pass out. I have an early morning
tomorrow." After expressing to me that he completely
understood, that he'd had a wonderful evening with
me and that he would love to do it again sometime very
soon, I forced my very last smile for him and said
goodnight, got in my car and drove the hell off.

See me again where? HA! In traffic maybe if he was
lucky.

May God bless our girlfriends; because through the ups, the downs, the great times, the horrible times, and even the most embarrassing of times...
we absolutely need our girlfriends by our sides every single step of the way.

♥

4

BFFs

"No he did not!" Angel blurted out through laughter as we sat in the busy downtown restaurant the next day eating lunch. I took a sip of my coffee and stared at her blankly. "Bitch it's not funny." I said sourly. "Bitch, yes the fuck it is!!" I rolled my eyes and shook my head. "I am never letting you or any other of you heifas talk me into ANYTHING ever again. Ugh. I'm so turned off. Fuck this dating shit."

Angel composed herself and smiled at me. "Oh stop it B. It was one bad experience. And it could have been worse... you could have slept with him and had bad sex. Now *that* would have been horrible." She took a sip of her Mimosa.

"Is sex all you ever think about Angel?"

"Yes B. It is. And once you start getting some good dick in your life again, it'll be all you ever think about too. Okay?" I started laughing and shook my head again.

"Actually. When was the last time you even had sex?" she asked. I thought about it for a second. "Uumm.. well..."

"Oh my God B. Don't tell me it's been *that* long since someone laid you on your back and gave it to you good."

"Angel can you stop worrying about my vagina please? She's good. I'm good. We're good!" — "Bullshit." She spat. "Next subject please." I said. "Fine. Wanna hit the club tonight?"

"No." I answered quickly. She waved a hand in the air dismissing my answer. "Anyways. I'm not even asking you—I'm telling you. *We* are hittin' the club tonight." She said. "Santiago is hosting a party over at Muzik and I know it's gonna be poppin' SO..." she raised her eyebrows and clapped her hands together—"Me and the rest of the squad are gonna come through your spot around 8pm. YOU are gonna go in that damn closet of yours and pick out sumin' seeexxxxy. Then I too am gonna go into that damn closet of yours and pick out sumin' sexy, because you got a bunch of sexy shit in there that still have the damn tags on em, because you never wear the shit you buy and you're so annoying; and then *we* are gonna hit that club lookin' like the black girl version of Sex In City and we're gonna make ALL these muthafuckas drool."

The waiter stopped at our table to ask if we needed anything, and Angel ordered another Mimosa while I rubbed my temples. "I hope you know that if we're Sex In The City, then you're Samantha." I said.

"Samantha is my spirit animal B." She retorted, batting her eyelashes. "I'd call you Carrie, but Carrie gets dick sooo..." I sat back in my chair smiling. "Maaan, why are we friends again?"

"Because I'm the one who's gonna show you how to get your damn groove back fool." She snapped her fingers and then pointed at me. "So be grateful." I shook my head and we both fell out laughing.

What oh what would my life be without my Angel.

Just because you've forgiven someone and moved on, doesn't mean that you ever forget exactly what they've done, and exactly how that shit felt.

♥

5

Pep Talks

"I'm not coming anymore." I told Jazzy on the phone an hour before she and the rest of the girls were supposed to be at my place.

"What? What do you mean you're not coming anymore? Girl stop it."

"Nah, I'm serious." I replied. "I just got wind that you know who is going to be at that party and I know he's gonna see me and go out of his way to smooth talk me into just hearing him out, and honestly... I don't know if I'll be strong enough to say no to his face. I haven't seen him in forever and I'd rather keep it that way. Blocking his number and all that was easy—well not easy but you know what I mean—but being face to face with him again? I just don't know if I'm up for that mentally."

I was dead ass serious too. I hadn't seen my ex since we'd broken up for good, and I just... I don't know.

Just hearing that we were going to be in the same room together made me uneasy—regardless of how big that room was or how many people were in it with us.

There was a long pause from Jazzy's end of the line.

"Jazz. You still there?"

"Girl, if you don't quit your shit!" She yelled. "What the fuck just happened? You been doing AMAZING. You been happy, you been glowing and shit. You been living your life and doing your own thing so how you gonna let that piece of shit fuckbag, fuck up your vibe like that? That's stupid—and you're *far* from stupid— so don't turn stupid on me now. So what if he's gonna be at the party—AND? Good. Let him be there. Even more reason for you to dress up like the fucking goddess that you are, and walk by his punk ass with your head high as fuck in the air. Let him be there and let his fucking black ass soul burn to ash as he watches you do your thing. And I wish a muhfucka WOULD try to talk to you, because I been waiting to cuss a bitch ass nigga like him out! So PLEASE let him try it. I dare him. 'Bout you're not coming out anymore... ANYWAYS. I'ma go ahead and act like this call never happened and we'll be at your place in an hour like we planned. In the meantime, I suggest you go stand in front of the mirror and remind yourself of the amazing woman you are, and how far you've come, and all the amazing things you've got going for yourself... and then take your ass in that shower and start getting ready. See you in a hour. Love you."

She hung up on before I could say another word.

Well damn.

I sat there on my bed and let Jazzy's words sink in. It wasn't that I wasn't over my ex as a person—because I was—but I don't think that I was 100 percent past all of the bad memories of what had happened between us yet. I still had a hint of a sour taste in my mouth whenever I was forced to think about him—and when I say forced I mean situations like these—because rarely did I ever think of him on my own time anymore.

I wouldn't say that I was still "hurting" but rather more uncomfortable with the idea of him.

All I knew for sure was that just as much as I didn't ever want to see him again, I didn't want him to ever see me again either. He was my past, and call me crazy but I wanted it to stay that way.

I got up from my bed and walked into my bathroom, and stood in front of my mirror to look at myself like Jazzy had suggested.

"What's your problem?" I asked my reflection. "You're in control. Remember? You've taken your life back. *You* are in control of you. Get a fucking grip B."

Tell a woman that she's nothing without you, and watch her turn around and become everything... without you.

♥

6

Squad

When my girls showed up at 10pm, I couldn't help but smile as they filed in the door. If there was one thing that I could honestly say about all of my friends, it would be that they were all drop dead fucking gorgeous.

Angel walked in first—the fucking Leo.

Angel had not one single filter on her mouth. If your skin wasn't thick, you would not survive around her for even an hour. Everything she thought in her mind, she would say out loud, and though it would get her (and us) into trouble sometimes, I always did admire and respect that about her. I'll admit that sometimes she would go overboard with her mouth though, because let's be honest here—not everything that we think always needs to be said out loud, and not everything that we think is always *right*—and Angel sometimes had issues with admitting or apologizing when she was wrong which was *heellllaaa* frustrating.

But, nonetheless, she always stood up for herself, never backed down from a confrontation and always stood firmly in her words...

I guess you could say that was her gift and her curse. And below that fucking mouth of hers, was an extremely good heart. If she loved you, she would give you the shirt off of her back on sight, and not a single person could ever speak badly about you in front of her without getting the cursing of their lifetime.

She was a real one all the way.

Her freshly dyed ash blonde hair sat evenly right at the top of her shoulders and was pressed bone straight. Everyone had told her before she dyed it not to, because it would wash out the tone of her skin (she was just a shade darker than my own caramel hue) but everyone was so so so wrong—she was rocking the shit out of that blonde hair, and out of all of the colors that she'd been through, it was by far my favorite.

Of course her face was beat for the whole heavens, as her smoky eyes were done perfectly and her clear lipgloss sat thick and luscious on her lips.

"Why are you wearing jeans?" I asked her, being a smart ass. "Heifa, don't get cute. I know I told you I was coming through your closet to get an outfit." She snapped as she walked past me into my bedroom.

Jazzy walked into the living room while Erika, holding a bottle of Pinot Noir, made her way into the kitchen. "Where's your wine opener B?" She called out. "First drawer under the microwave!" I hollered back.

Jazzy plopped down on the sofa and rubbed her feet. "Damn new shoes already fucking with me. I knew these were gonna be some two hour heels! Man I'ma suffer tonight. The shit we gotta go through to stay cute!"

Jazzy—a Pisces just like me. She was a giver and rarely a taker, with a huge heart that she wore on her sleeve, and constantly went out of her way for everyone—her gift and her curse. She was the one who could be dead asleep at 2am, but would answer her phone and listen if you called because you needed someone to vent to for three hours. She was the one that would reach out to hug you first if you started crying in front of her, and out of the four of us, she was hands down the ultimate fashionista. The type of girl who could wear a lime green skirt, with a bright ass pink blazer and rock the shit out of it. She lived, breathed and ate fashion everything.

She was also a name brand whore and everything she owned was designer (no seriously, everything) but ironically, she was also the most reserved out of the four of us—the introvert.

It was crazy to others because she dressed for all of the attention in the world, but wasn't anywhere close to being a social butterfly. I understood her though. I think that I may have been the only one who truly understood everything there was to understand about her, because we were pretty much exactly the same for the most part. (Except the hugging and the fashion thing. I wasn't the type to reach out and hug people like that all the time, and I was more of a simple dresser. A lot of blacks, dark blues and greens, whites and greys.)

Unlike Angel who was outspoken and didn't give a fuck who was around or not, Jazzy only spoke up and out when she was around people that she was comfortable with, and kept quiet and simply observed when new faces were around. But you know what they say about the quiet ones right?

Watch out.

Jazzy and I shared equal qualities that could easily frustrate other people: We both lived in our own little worlds half of the time. You know the type of people who could be staring dead in your face and not hear a fucking word you just said? That was us. Out of the four of us, Jazzy and I probably spent the most time snapping our fingers in each others face talking about "hello? Are you fucking listening?"—frustrating to others, yes, but not when it came to dealing with each other.

"Where did you get that pant suit?" I asked her. "It's extra dope!" It was a satin royal blue, and complimented her cocoa colored skin perfectly. With a deep plunge line in the front, and completely open in the back, it hugged the top half of her body and her full C-cup breasts perfectly, and then loosened up right at the beginning of her tiny hips.
She smiled and winked at me, as she pushed her light brown curls away from her face. "Girl you know I stay with the hook-ups. I got it at this dope little hidden place downtown. I'll take you next week if you want. They've got stuff in there that you'll for sure love."

That was another great thing about Jazzy—she *always* had the hook-ups.

"Someone explain to me why the hell B isn't dressed yet?" Erika said as she came out of the kitchen with four wine glasses and the bottle, purposely talking as if I wasn't standing right damn there.

Erika was the wild card of the squad—a Gemini. You just never fucking knew what she was going to be on any given day, and yes, I do mean *what.* Sometimes she was hella peace and love, and other days, she could burn someone's house down to the ground and not even bat an eyelash as she stayed and watched. Some days she was really quiet, other days you'd think she was a talk show host running her mouth, and because of that, she often rubbed many people the wrong way. Though she was a coin toss in the air when it came to her moods, and could be extremely exhausting and draining to anyone because of them, she was ride or die for her girls without question. Nothing came before us and she would drop anything that did come along, for us.

Erika's skin was a beautiful deep shade of chocolate brown. I *loved* the color of her skin. Matter of fact, I remember the first time I had ever met her, "your skin is fucking beautiful" were the very first words out of my mouth. She was average height and hit the gym like it was her religion, so her entire body was tight as fuck and her booty sat perfectly high and round behind her. Her skin-tight long sleeved white ribbed dress hit half way between her ankles and knees, and her pressed jet black hair fell just a little bit above her average sized breasts. The only makeup she wore was a dark pink lipstick and long feathery lashes, but trust me when I say that she didn't need anything else.

"It won't take me long to get ready y'all know that." I answered taking the bottle from Erika. "Lemme open this before you fuck around and splatter some of it on your dress." She pursed her lips and pointed her finger at me. "Good call B."

"I smell alcohol being opened in there!" Angel yelled out.

"Girl mind yo damn nose and get dressed!" Jazzy yelled back. "And B, gimme that and go get ready wit yo slow ass." She took the bottle from me and I rolled my eyes as Angel stepped into the room wearing a strapless dark red mini dress of mine that I had never worn, with a pair of nude pumps that she'd brought with her, and matching clutch. We were the exact same size and shape, so the dress fit her like it was her own.

She stopped in front of us and placed a hand on her hip dramatically. "I... am ready." she said, and then eyed me.

"Alright, alright! I'm going to go get ready now! Damn."

An hour and a two glasses of wine later, I was ready to go. I emerged from my bedroom and Jazzy whistled.

"Well *helllooooo* goddess!"

I had on a black see-through lace dress that hit my knees, with a matching silk slip underneath that stopped an inch above them, and a sexy pair of six inch black stilettos with gold cuffs that gripped my ankles. I had slicked my hair into a ponytail that hung right to the middle of my back and of course, my favorite deep crimson matte lipstick was painted on my lips, while my black eyeliner sat winged to perfection on top of my full set of lashes.

"Well shit girl!" Angel said smiling, "Someone's gonna ask you to marry them tonight with all that sexy mixed with class you've got goin' on!" I blushed and smiled back. "Y'all ready?" I asked. And as my three girls stood up, I shook my head. "Damn it we look gooooood."

I think that every woman needs a time-out in her life to just do her own thing without compromise or regret. Just a time-out in her life when, for once, she puts herself first.

♥

7
All Eyes On Us

We pulled up at the club and the line up was literally
wrapped around the block.

"Um. I know we ain't standing in that. Someone
please tell me that we are not muthafuckin' standing in
that line." Jazzy begged. "Girl please. You know damn
well Santiago put us on the list and got us a table."
Angel answered. "And even if he didn't, you know
damn well that we don't do fucking lineups." I added.

We parked and headed to the front of the line where
the first few girls who were waiting _in_ the line, instantly
started throwing daggers at us through their eyes.
"Haters." Erika mumbled. I shot her a stern look.
"Don't you start." I wasn't in the mood for _any_ drama
whatsoever, and sometimes, Erika could be a shit
disturber.

Angel gave our names to the big husky mean ass
looking doorman who was guarding the door, and

immediately, he called for a host to walk us through
the crowd and to our table—now that's the shit I like.

The club was already bumpin' and our table was
perfectly positioned in a section all to ourselves.
Santiago had hooked us up the real way, and I was
ready to let loose and have myself a good ass time.
A waitress quickly came over to take care of us and we
ordered a bottle Veuve Clicquot and a bottle of VSOP.

All eyes were on us when the bottles came and people
started to realize that it was just us four at the table.
Normally wherever there were bottles, well, there were
men. But my squad and I were different. None of us
were into that "find a dude with a table in the VIP and
drink off of his bottles" shit. And none of us were into
standing around at the fucking bar, waiting to flag
down the bartender to buy single drinks all while
trying to explain to random dudes that came pushing
up beside us, that we weren't interested.

Fuck that.

We all made our own good money in life, so we could
afford to go out and do things our way. Plus, this way
we got to have a good time and pick and choose which

dudes we wanted to pay attention to, *if* we felt like paying attention to any at all. Know what I mean?

An hour into the party and I was getting a little tipsy. Not like 'I need to sit down' tipsy, but a nice vibe type of tipsy. I was with my girls, we were fly as fuck, we were laughing and dancing, I was feeling myself, the DJ was dropping good music and the energy in the place was on point. I was enjoying myself for real.

Our waitress came back over and rubbed my arm gingerly, and I leaned in to hear what she wanted to tell me. "What kind of bottle would you like for your table?" She asked. I looked at her confused. "Um, we already have two bottles on our table." She smiled and this time leaned into me. "I know, but that guy over there is offering you a bottle. Anything you want he said—so don't be shy."

More confusion on my face. "Which guy?"

She pointed to the VIP across from us almost on the other side of the club. "The one in the red shirt looking over here." I followed her finger with my eyes across the room and squinted to try to get a look at his face.

"What's going on?" Angel yelled over the music. The waitress repeated to her what she had said to me, and Angel smacked my arm. "Girl you better take that damn bottle! Don't you know who that is?" I turned and looked at her. "No."

She rolled her eyes. "How do you not know who that... know what I'll tell you later." She turned her attention back toward the waitress—"You can bring us a bottle of Ace Of Spades please."

"Bitch are you crazy?!" I yelled. "We are not ordering a nine hundred dollar fucking bottle of champagne on that man's tab! What's wrong with you?" I looked at the waitress and smiled, "tell him I said thank you very much for the kind gesture, but we're good." Jazzy and Erika were now in the mix and were looking at Angel and I for some answers. "Nathan just sent a waitress over here offering B a bottle of whatever she wants, and she's tryna turn it down."

Jazzy's eyes grew wide. "WHAT?!" She screeched in my face, "girl if you don't smarten your ass up right now!"

"That's what I said!" Angel exclaimed.

"Guys?" I was getting frustrated. "WHO THE FUCK IS NATHAN?!" Erika turned to the waitress calmly, "we'll take the Ace Of Spades. Thank you." The waitress smiled and rushed back into the crowd. I turned to Erika, "Why would you just do that?" I asked. "Why would you ever say no to Nathan?" She asked me back. "Okay, if someone doesn't tell me who the fuck Nathan is and why the fuck I should give a shit, I'm going home RIGHT now. Y'all are working my nerves."

"Nathan is a friend of Santiago's" Angel explained over the music. "He's the type of guy that everyone can't help but notice when he walks in the room, because he's sexy as fuck, hella polite and just looks like money, but he's quiet and keeps to himself. Every girl wants him—literally—but he doesn't really pay them any attention like that. So if he has his eye on you, that means you've caught his attention, the real way."

As Angel spoke, I was still trying to squint my eyes to get a good look at his face.
This shit *would* happen the one night I decide not to wear my contacts.

The waitress came back with our bottle, some fresh flute glasses, and set things up. "Well if he wants *my* attention the *real* way, he's gonna have to do a little bit more than send a bottle over here because clearly I can buy my own bottles. But I am gonna go over there and at least say thank you to him, and probably apologize on behalf of my *thirsty* ass friends for ordering the most expensive damn bottle in the club." I told Angel rolling my eyes. "I'll be right back."

I stepped down out of our VIP booth and started sexy-walking my way towards his, and as I neared it, he turned and faced me.

Angel was not lying when she said that this man was fine as fuck.

I hadn't even reached him yet and could already see how soft the skin on his milk chocolate face was. He had no facial hair, but the hair on his head was cut in a very low fade with an impeccably clean outline.

He was dressed simple—a fitted red t-shirt, black jeans and black Gucci sneakers—and unlike all of his boys who were wearing enough jewelry for me to buy a car with, all he wore was a gold watch. Overly flashy men were the ultimate turnoff for me, so I appreciated his simple style right away. My plan was to introduce myself, let him formally introduce himself, say thank you for the bottle and then go to the bathroom, because Jesus Christ did I ever have to pee. But right as I was getting ready to step into his booth, I felt a hand grab mine. I turned around swiftly and looked up, and that's when my heart fell to my heels.

It was my ex.

Fuck. Fuck. Fuck. Fuck. Fuck. Fuck.

The moment our eyes met, I panicked and felt sick at the same time—I needed air.

I quickly pulled my hand away from his and without saying a word, made my way to the exit instead of to Nathan.

I can't do this right now. I can't. There's just no way.

I've learned that it's important to surround yourself with people who will have your back, and stand strong for you, in moments where you're having trouble standing strong for yourself.

♥

8

True Love

I had never in my life pushed through a crowd of people so fucking quickly, and once I made it outside, I silently cursed myself because I realized that my car keys were in Jazzy's purse—so where the fuck was I really going?

"B! Stop! I just want to talk to your for a minute." I heard him yelling from behind me.

Shit. Just keep walking B. Keep walking.

"B?! Would you stop? What's your problem?"

What was _my_ problem?

Oh I stopped alright. In an instant, my brain had gone from _panic_ mode to _wait a minute... you need to tell him to go fuck himself_ mode, and I spun around on my heels facing him.

"YOU are my fucking problem!" I suddenly yelled. "YOU. ARE. MY. FUCKING. PROBLEM."

I was so mad. Why couldn't he just see me, and leave me alone? Why did he have to touch me? Why did he have to acknowledge me at all? Why did he have to come running out of the fucking club yelling behind me in the middle of the street like the selfish prick that he clearly still was? *Why?*

"You're my fucking problem so GO AWAY. I don't want to see you. I don't want to hear you. I don't..."

"B.." he interrupted. "NO!" I spat.

"B, *NOTHING.* YOU SHUT YOUR MOUTH."

How dare he fucking cut me off right now, is he stupid?!

"I don't want to see you." I started over again in a much lower tone. "I don't want to hear you. I don't want you to find ways to call or text me. I don't even want to know that you still exist on this planet—do you get that? I want you to leave me alone." As I spoke the words through gritted teeth and a shaky voice, I stared right into his eyes, even though my eyes were starting to blur with tears. "Go back inside the club." I told him. He stared at me and shook his head. "Man, you have some serious issues."

Typical.

Typical for a man of his kind to cold heartedly, and purposely drag a woman through piles and piles of BULLSHIT, and then tell her that *she*'s the one with issues when she doesn't want to see his face ever again.

Fucking typical.

"No. I don't have issues. I have AN issue—just ONE—and it's *you* standing in my fucking presence. So can you please, for the millionth time, get the entire FUCK. OUT. OF. MY. LIFE." I turned my back towards him and started walking down the street.

"B! B! Hold up!" This time it was Jazzy's voice hollering at me. I turned and watched her as she pushed past my fucking issue who was still standing there like an idiot. "Oh that's right." he sneered. "Here we go. Go ahead and get on your little women empowerment shit and have your little group meeting with your girls now, and cry about how much of a *bad guy* I was." Before I could say anything at all, Jazzy—without warning—flipped the fuck out.

"Nigga? Are you for real right now? You ARE A BAD GUY and you're THE WORST kind of bad guy there is! You had a girl who was *soooo* fucking good to you. Do you even know how many men would have LOVED to be in your place? Do you even know how many men I watched this girl constantly shut the fuck down while she was with you? And GOOD men might I add. AMAZING men. Men that wanted nothing more than to put a fucking ring on her finger and give her the world. She cooked for you everyday. You had a clean house. She fucked you all the time. Sucked your dick all the time. She supported you AND your little bitch ass dreams—which by the way were, and still are, WACK. With her, you were living the life of a fucking King."

She started walking towards him, and I can't even lie, I got a little scared. It had been a really long time since I'd seen her that angry and going the fuck off.

I tried to grab her arm to pull her back towards me and she shook me off. "No B. Fucking enough is enough.

Now *I've* had enough." She turned her attention back towards him and kept going.

"You didn't deserve her then, and you sure as hell don't deserve even a *conversation* from her now. You really don't. And it's sad, because she loved you so fucking much and you can't help who you love, so she kept trying to hang on because she had all of this faith. She *really* believed in that big fucking heart of hers, that if she just hung in there, you'd come around and see her for the extra dope woman that she is. But you? You just kept fucking up. Kept cheating. Kept having her out here looking crazy. Kept playing games with her mind and fucking with her emotions. You single handedly disrupted her sense of security to the point where she ended up feeling like she wasn't good enough. Wasn't worthy enough. You had her really believing for so long that there was something wrong with *her* when really, it was YOU. There was, and obviously still very much is, something fucking wrong with YOU."

I was silent. I didn't know what the fuck to say and for the first time since we had been outside, I took a look around me and realized that there were a bunch of people watching us.

We were making a scene, and I immediately felt embarrassed—I sincerely hated public scenes like that. My piece of shit ex and my girl were standing head to head and I couldn't believe that he hadn't said a word throughout her entire abusive word vomit.

"Let's just go girl." I said pulling her by the arm. She was still staring at him, almost as if she was silently daring him to say something. "Come on." I pleaded, and this time she complied, turned around and started walking with me. I heard him start to laugh and shout out from behind us, "I GUESS THAT'S WHAT FRIENDS ARE FOR RIGHT!"

"Don't even bother to respond." Jazzy said. "Let's just keep walking before I fucking actually jump him. I've got your keys. Let's go to the car."

You know, I didn't realize until that very moment, that all of the shit that I'd been through with him had weighed on her too, and to the point where *she* couldn't even take it anymore. It's crazy how we women will go through our lives saying shit like—"this is my life and what I do or who I'm with is none of anyone else's business." But the truth is, what we do affects the ones around us... especially the ones we call friends.

We run to our friends for everything—the good times, the bad times, the embarrassing times and the exciting times. We run to them when we're nervous, scared, or vulnerable and need a shoulder to lean on or to cry on. We count on them to cheer us up and make us laugh, and we give them our secrets to hold onto forever. We run to our friends for *everything*.

So how dare we think for a second that the things that we go through, don't affect them too? How dare we run to them, but then turn around and tell them to mind their own business? If the shit we went through didn't bother them at all—then why the fuck would we call them friends?

We walked silently, but hand in hand, until we got to my car and then Jazzy broke the ice. "B, my bad for losing it like that. Like, I know that's your business with him and I shouldn't have put my mouth in it but I ..."

I waved my hand cutting her off.

"Honestly, please don't even apologize because I don't know what I would have done or said or *not said* if you weren't there speaking for me. All you did was tell the truth; and the truth is, he didn't ever deserve me at all.

I don't even know why I let him get a rise out of me to begin with and I'm so mad at myself for letting that happen. You were right about what you said earlier on the phone—I have been doing great and I have been feeling on top of the world. But seeing him, even though I have forgiven him for everything, is still like looking at the devil."

She nodded her head in agreement. "I feel you B. I'll be honest, I fucking hate him for you and I always have, even while you were with him. Everything I said to him has been inside of me for so long I swear. I have been *dying* to just let him have a piece of my mind but I didn't think it was gonna be out in the open yelling like a crazy bitch in the streets!" She let out a soft laugh.

"Nah, it's all good. Thank you Jazz. Thank you for being strong for me while I was having trouble being strong for myself." A tear slid down my face and she pulled me close to her, hugging me tightly, as I started to cry uncontrollably. I don't even know where the tears came from. Maybe the liquor mixed with the intensity of the moment, mixed with the love I had for Jazzy, mixed with the frustration from what had just happened with that asshole—had my already sensitive ass *extra* sensitive. "I gotchu B." She whispered in my ear. "I got your back. Always have and always will. That's my word."

If there was ever a thing that my ex was right about, it was his comment about friends.

This was *exactly* what friends were for.

. . .

I got home home, peeled off my dress and tossed it in the dry cleaning pile, slid out of my panties and tossed them in the laundry pile, then headed to the shower.

I stood under the hot water and thought about the night and all that had transpired, and instead of questioning it and getting upset at myself all over again for reacting the way that I did—I decided to just close my eyes, and pray.

I prayed for my girls, I prayed for my family...

and then I prayed for myself.

Sometimes, the most valuable lesson that a man can ever teach you is that you can do better... than him.

♥

9
<u>Seize The Opportunity</u>

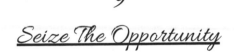

Believe it or not, despite the mess of the night before, I awoke the next morning feeling refreshed. I layed there thinking of all of my girls, and how grateful I truly was to have them in my life. I thought about my ex too just a little bit and I shuddered—some people just never change, and he was still an asshole.

It did suck that the night ended the way that it did though. Erika and Angel were pissed that they were still in the club while all of the drama was going down and that no one called them to come out, but it was better that way, and this I knew. While Jazzy used her words as weapons, I knew that had Angel and Erika been in the mix, they would have used hands. Definitely wouldn't have been, or ever is, the right action to take... but I knew my girls.

I sat up in my bed and stretched when my phone chimed on the dresser beside me. *"Hangover brunch in an hour at my place."* The text from Erika read.

"Bet." I wrote back.

. . .

"Soooo, can we just take a moment to talk about how fucking fine Nathan is? And how bad he wants B though?" Angel asked pouring some coffee into her mug.

With all of the commotion Nathan was the furthest thing from my mind, but as she said his name, an image of his flawless face popped up in my memory. I took a bite of my bagel and smiled. "He is fine." I agreed. "I left that damn club so quick I didn't even have a chance to say shit to him and really feel him out."
My girls exchanged glances and sly grins together.
"Girl, you know I had to slip him your digits before I left." Erika confessed.
I looked at them and blinked my eyes. "What?"

"I mean damn, it's NATHAN! Shit, I couldn't just let that opportunity pass you by."

"See, now why you gotta call him an opportunity?" I asked. "Dick opportunity B." Angel interjected. "He's a dick opportunity. Would you please follow along. Damn."

I sighed a long sigh. "I do need some dick gawt damn it." My girls started clapping and Angel got up for a standing ovation. "YAAAS! Finally! Shit. Admitting it is the first step girl."

"Shut *up.*" I laughed.

"Shit, I've been so busy tryna get you some new dick these past couple months, I haven't had time to scout for my own." Angel said. I was confused. "Huh? But what happened to what's his name? I thought things were going good between y'all."

She took a sip of her coffee and shrugged her shoulders.

"Yea they were. They were going great until his true colors started to show a bit, and I know better now than to ignore someone's true colors—feel me? I ain't putting myself in no more fucked up situations—only removing myself from them, and I removed myself from that one with the quickness. There's plenty of men out there girl... ain't nobody got time to be worried about one who ain't fitting my mould, or to be trying to force anyone to fit it either. These men need to step up to my level, cause I for damn sure ain't stooping down to theirs. I'm queening out here. I need someone who's kinging."

"AMEN! My sista AMEN." Erika yelled. "Shit, I'ma second that." Jazzy said. "I mean, how could I not third that!" I chimed in.

That was Angel for you though. If there was anyone on this planet who did not have time for the bullshit—it was her. She would drop a dude in a heartbeat without even telling him why, and then keep it moving like he never happened.

Angel was *life*.

"Erika. When are you going to introduce us to your little boo thang?" Jazzy asked switching gears. Erika was sitting at the table in an old t-shirt eight sizes too big for her, with wild hair. She smiled and shrugged her shoulders like a teenager in love. "When the time is right." she said softly. "I have to make sure that this is going to be a real person in my life before I start bringing him around my actual real people—you know?" We all nodded.

Unlike the rest of us, Erika was really secretive when it came to the men she dated. She didn't like to talk too much about things until they were secured. "I don't wanna jinx shit" she would always say. I felt her though. I really did. We had all been through so much shit and had our fair share of bleeding hearts when it came to men, so I didn't blame her for wanting to be extra cautious. Plus, you know how it is when you bring a dude around your girls— it's like putting him on the stand in front of a jury and having to wait until they all reach a decision unanimously—and we all know that part, too soon, can send a dude running in the other direction, and I could tell by the way Erika's eyes lit up every time we mentioned her *boo thang* that she was really feeling him. So I would always fall back on the subject and just let her do her thing at her own pace.

As we were sitting around the table eating and laughing while re-caping the good parts of the night, my phone started ringing. I looked at the screen and screwed up my face. "Who's that?" Angel asked with her nosey self.

"No clue, I don't know this number."

"Well answer it fool! Maybe it's Nathan."

I wiped my hand on the side of my sweat pants, hit the answer button then hit the speakerphone button.

"Hello good afternoon." I said.

"Hello good afternoon. Is this B?"

All of my girls jumped up excitedly at the sound of the the sexy deep voice that responded back to me, and I can't even lie—my heart kinda skipped a beat too. I couldn't help but to grin while I started waving my hands in the air motioning for everyone to sit the fuck down and shut up. "Yes, this is she." I replied in my most sophisticated voice, while Jazzy gave me the *'bitch you know damn well your voice don't really sound like that'* look.

I put my middle finger up to her.

"Who is this please?"

"This is Nathan. I hope I'm not catching you at a bad time, and I do apologize right off the bat if you feel like this phone call may be a little bit intrusive, as I never did get a chance to formally introduce myself last night, because you disappeared. Your homegirl Erika gave me your number, but if you are offended by my call I will completely understand and respect that."

Damn he was good.

"No, no." I said. "I'm not offended at all, and I appreciate you starting the conversation in that manner. Very gentlemanly of you."

"The moment I saw you walk in the club, I couldn't take my eyes off you. I watched the way you carried yourself up until the very moment you vanished, and I knew right away that you weren't like most girls out here. I could tell you were a lady. So I'm going to treat you like one."

"Oooooouuuu giiirrrlllllllll" Angel whispered as she reached over and smacked me on the shoulder. I blushed and smacked her back.

"That is very sweet of you. I like that." I said into the phone.

"I'm a very sweet guy B, but only for the right woman."

"Well you got yo'self a smooth-talker on yo hands girl." Jazzy said quietly. "Would y'all two chatterboxes shut the hell up until the phone call is over?" Erika scolded. "Good God."

Angel and Jazzy giggled, and Nathan continued—"And this is nothing by the way. I can show you a lot sweeter if you let me."

Like I said before—I wasn't swearing off all men. I wanted my life to be full of fun and excitement, and whoever wanted to add to that... then I was all for it. I knew my girls wouldn't have ever given my number to some piece of shit idiot, so I was confident that I didn't have anything to worry about. Plus, there was not one red flag being waved by my intuition—only green ones.

If Nathan wanted to show me some sweet *thangs*, I was down to let him.

Let's go.

I have a strong love for things that never go out of style—like tender gentlemen, classy women, red lipstick, and the color black.

♥

10

Queen B

Jesus fuck Nathan was *fiiiiiine.*

It had been a couple of months since the day of his first phone call, and we had been kickin' it at least once a week ever since. He wasn't only hella easy on the eyes, but he was dope as fuck over all, and I was having a blast with him.

He had a thing for trying new restaurants, good art and live Jazz—and I *loved* to eat, I could definitely appreciate some good art, and I LOVED live Jazz clubs—so our dates were literally always the best.

Nathan wasn't pushy and all up on me, and I liked that very much. He respected my space, my busy work schedule, and never overstepped the boundaries that I put in place. I wasn't the text all day or stay on the phone for hours every day type of girl—I had my own life and my own things going on, and I just didn't have the time for that. I liked simple shit. I was the type of girl who liked to check in here and there throughout the week, and then catch up face to face, and I think he really liked that about me too.

Most of the time he would send a text that said something quick and smooth like, "Are you tryna be in the lobby of your building in a sexy dress at 8pm tonight?" And I would giggle and blush like a damn schoolgirl reading it, and reply, "You damn right I am."

He was never late. Never once did I reach that lobby and have to wait even a second for him to pull up in his clean all black Range Rover, and when I would walk out to the car, he would always be standing beside the passenger door ready to open it for me—I'm telling you, he was smooth as shit. He made me feel like the Queen of the everything, and after all I had been through in the years before, I fucking deserved to be treated like the damn Queen that I was for a change.

Have I mentioned how damn good he always smelled?

Lawd.

He would lean in to give me a kiss on the cheek and maaaaan... I would just want to whip my panties at him on the spot.

To keep it all the way real, I'd reached a point where I was constantly drifting off into my own imagination with him, and it was becoming my new favorite thing to do. Picturing how his lips would feel traveling up and down my inner thighs. How his body would move in rhythm with mine. What his moans would sound like in my ear as he thrusted in and out of me on a mission to make me cum—and I wanted to cum for him oh so fucking badly—but I was nervous, and shy as fuck. I hadn't had sex with anyone since my ex, and while I wanted to embark in the whole 'no strings attached' thing... I guess I wasn't exactly sure how to go about it without complicating shit, because no matter how dope he was, me not wanting an actual boyfriend was still very much a real thing. Feel me?

This part of my life was still brand new to me and I didn't want to fuck it up, but at the same time, I was torturing myself... which was dumb.

I was a grown ass woman.
He was a grown ass man.
I had needs.
He had needs.

Why the fuck was I denying myself of my damn needs?

I was gonna fuck the entire soul out of Nathan one of these days—he just didn't know it yet.

Learning where to place people—and how to keep them in their fucking places.

♥

II

Bye Felicia

Saturday morning.

"Yo." I started typing into our group chat. "Nathan's boy is having some birthday bash tonight in some club that I can't remember the name of. #Anywaythough he invited me and my squad. Y'all rolling or what?"

It didn't even take four seconds for Angel to reply "FUCK. YES." followed by Jazzy and Erika's "I'm down."

I sent an "lol" and then wrote "bet. Let's dooo this."

I put my phone down and was reminded quickly of the two broken nails that I had from slamming my fingers in the car door earlier that morning.

"Fuuuck my life." I said out loud while throwing my head back. I couldn't go out with two ugly ass broken nails, there was just no way, so I called my nail shop and prayed to God that they could take me on such a busy day with such little notice.

. . .

The nail shop was extremely busy as I walked in for my appointment and it immediately annoyed me. It was a quick reminder of why I always avoided doing my nails on a Saturday. I just so happen to be one of those people who hates bumping into random folks that I don't talk to on a regular basis, or care to talk to all, and that shop in particular was a popular one in our area of town—so literally *everyone* went there, and *everyone* did their nails on Saturday.

My favorite nail tech (and the ONLY one that I would let touch my nails) signaled for me to sit in his chair. The place was crowded and loud, and as I made my way over to sit, I spotted three familiar faces sitting over in the pedicure chairs and just as quickly as I had spotted them, was just as quickly as I pretended to have *not* seen them. But unfortunately for me, they saw me too.

"B!" One of them shouted staring right at me.
All the other women in the salon turned to look at me, and I cringed.

Like must you be SO loud? I thought.
Is it absolutely necessary to shout my fucking name from clear across the room and draw all this attention?

I looked up and waved at all three of them forcing the entire fuck out of a believable smile. "Oh hey y'all. What's up?" *God, please make this exchange of words between us very short and very sweet. Please?*

"Nothing guuuurl, haven't seen you in a good while! Where have you been hiding?!"

Just fuck off.

"Oh you know, just doing my thing." I replied as I sat down in the chair. I pulled out my phone and started scrolling through it randomly, hoping she would take the hint and STOP TALKING FOREVER... but some people in life, just don't fucking pick up on hints.

"Doing your *thaaang* huh. I hear that girl. I definitely hear that. Do you still talk to ol' boy and stuff?"—there it was. The inquiry about my ex.
The million dollar question.

The million *fucking* dollar question that TWO whole years later, people *still* had the nerve to ask me... and why? EVERYONE knew the fucking answer. It had been the talk of the damn city two years ago so it just boggled my mind that people still just *had* to ask. Every time they bumped into me it was as if they couldn't help themselves. Like, why ask a person who you don't even kick it, about shit that has nothing to do with you? Fucking *why?*

Gossip Queens man. I hated them.

I hated them, and I fucking hated the nail shop on Saturdays.

I composed myself on the inside and then answered dryly, but politely—"No. I do not." And then looked back into my phone. Think she would pick up on hint number two? Nope. She pressed on.

"Like you don't speak to him *at all*, at all?"

Oh my God, Oh my God. Dear heavenly father please hold my hand by my side to keep me from slapping the shit out this bitch because I do not belong in jail.

"Nope. Not at all." I answered politely, again. Other people in the shop were starting to pay attention to our conversation and it was really bothering me. "So he hasn't even tried to reach out? Because you know how niggas are, they fuck up and then they tr..."

"Are you fucking him now or something?" I cut her off, annoyed as fuck, and unable to hold myself back any longer. Completely taken aback, her mouth dropped to the floor. "What?"
I rephrased my question and lifted my voice a good four levels. "Are *you* having *sexual intercourse* with *my* ex?"

Well, if *all* of the people in the place weren't already listening to the conversation, please believe that now every pair of eyes and ears were focused on us as I stared at her, and only her.

"No I'm not sleeping with... why would you.. I mean where would that even come from?"

"Nah, I'm just asking. Because I don't see why else you would be so completely pressing about a situation that has absolutely nothing-to-fucking-do with you—feel me?" I could tell that I had stunned her and she was searching her mind for something to say. So before she found her words, I figured I would keep going and really let her fucking have a piece of my mind since she wanted it so badly anyway.

"Like let's be real here—you and I are not friends. We don't kick it, we don't call each other, and we don't look out for each other. We see each other from time to time and say 'what's up' simply because we have mutual friends, grew up in the same hood, and we've worked together in the same establishment once upon a time—but we're not friends. So what's it to you whether *my* ex boyfriend has, or has not, reached out to me? Why are you even asking me anything at all? Unless you're fucking him now and just want to make sure that he's not still in contact with me."

The entire shop was blanketed in an uncomfortable/awkward energy, and her two little sidekick friends had their heads down embarrassed for her. "I am not sleeping with your ex." She said again.

"Oh good!" I said clapping my hands together. "So now that we've gotten that out the way, I can go ahead and say that whatever did, didn't, is, or isn't going on between him and I, is *none* of your fucking concern—right?" My nail tech walked over and sat down in front of me breaking the force field between her and I, then took my hand to start my nails but gave it a little rub first. Like a 'take a deep breathe and just ignore her' type of rub.

"My bad B." she said with half of an attitude. "I didn't mean to be all up in your shit like that." I moved my head so that I could look at her one last time and said, "Oh no no. My name is Cici, so you can refer to me as that. Only my friends call me B."

My nail tech cracked a smiled and gave me a wink as he filed my nails. I heard her mumbled something under her breath and start talking shit to her girls and I shook my head. "See why I don't like coming in this bitch on Saturdays?" I asked him.

I'm a dope ass woman, with a dope ass heart, and I'm not going to keep denying others of my dopeness just because one asshole wasn't able to comprehend what he had—fuck that.

♥

12

Baby Got Plans

We met up at Jazzy's place this time and decided to take her car. I was always the designated driver and that night, well...

let's just say I wanted to have more than two drinks.

My girls were already waiting for me beside Jazzy's car as I pulled up because of course—I was running late as usual. I parked across the street then sashayed over to them.

Erika whistled when she saw me, while Jazzy and Angel started yelling cat calls.

"Damn maaa!"

"You not even playing tonight!"

"Where did you get that dress?"

"And those heels! Gurl, YAS! Come through! You are fucking everything right now!"

Yes, that night I was everything on purpose, because that was the night I wanted Nathan to understand that he was taking me home with him.
Though I probably had a good 20 new dresses sitting in my closet that had never been worn, and heels that still hadn't ever hit pavement, I wanted new everything for that night. So after I finished my nails, I went straight to the mall and had myself a little spree.
New dress, new heels, new clutch, new perfume, new watch, new *everythang* except panties—those weren't going to be apart of my attire for the evening.

I was wearing an Olive green suede dress with the tiniest spaghetti straps in the world, that hit right below my knees and had a deep open back that stopped right above the crack of ass. It hugged my body like it was custom made for me and the color complimented my caramel skin perfectly. I had slightly waved my hair with the curling wand and had left it loose to cascade all the way down my back, and my pointy-toed stilettos were a soft shade of gold matching my watch and my clutch.

Because I wanted the color of my dress to be the focal point of the entire look, I traded my usual crimson lipstick for a nude lip color that matched my complexion, and opted for a dark brown smokey eye over my lids.

I stood in front of my girls, flipped my hair for dramatics and smiled coyly at them.

"I *meaaaan*, sometimes a girl's gotta switch it up a bit."

"Oh fuck nah. That nigga Nathan is gonna get you pregnant tonight FOR. SURE! We gotta stop at the store real quick and get you some condoms." Angel said, and we all burst out laughing.

. . .

The club was lit, and as usual, we were in the VIP turning the fuck up. Angel had her eye on one of Nathan's boys, so she was over beside him flirting her life away, while Jazzy and Erika were in their own little world vibing to the music and enjoying the energy, while I couldn't take my eyes off of Nathan, and he never took his eyes off of me.

"I really, really like that skirt on you." He said.

Men.

Don't know the difference between a damn dress and a skirt.

I looked down at my *dress* and then back up at him and shot him a devilish smirk. "What if I told you that I wasn't wearing any panties underneath it?" It was the first time I had ever spoken to him in a sexual manner like that, and a slow smile spread across his perfect lips.

God I loved his fucking lips.

Instantly understanding what I wanted him to understand, and going with my flow, he leaned closer to me and whispered—"Well then I guess I would have to slide my hand under there to make sure you weren't lying. Now wouldn't I?"

I took his hand and placed it on my thigh. "I think you should definitely check to make sure I'm not lying." The feel of his hand against my bare skin was enough.

I wanted him.
I needed him.

Enough of this bullshit.

Fuck the club.
Fuck his friend's birthday party.

We needed to get the fuck out of there.

"I'm taking you home with me tonight." He said softly into my ear. I closed my eyes and bit the bottom of my lip, then leaned into his ear and purred—"No. You're taking me home with you right fucking now."

Magic words.

"Yo." I said tapping the girls on the shoulder and interrupting Angels flirt game. "I'm out, okay?" Angel grabbed me by my arm and pulled me close. "I would high five you, but I don't wanna make it obvious that I know you're gonna finally get some D."

Fucking Angel man.

"Y'all get home safe and text me!" I said grinning while pulling myself out of her grip.

Erika turned to Nathan and looked him directly in his eye. "I know I don't have to tell you this because you're not stupid, but I'ma say it anyways just incase, plus I'm half tipsy so... I don't give a fuck. If you break my girl's heart, I'm going to kick you in the dick Nathan—and I mean that. I will kick you in the dick and then do something awful to your car every time I see it. I am not playing. Do *not* fuck with my girl's heart. Do you understand me?"

Nathan took both of Erika's hands in his, and looked her right back in her eyes. "I would never fuck with such a beautiful thing. You have my word."

God bless my girls, because they loved the shit outta me, but Erika didn't have to worry about my heart because that wasn't what I was about to give to Nathan. My heart was the last thing on my mind...

Every now and then people come into your life and give you exactly what you need... exactly when you need it.

♥

13

After Midnight

As soon as he closed the door to his condo—it was on.

He took me swiftly in his arms and kissed me like he had been starving for me. The taste of his lips mixed with the hint of alcohol on his tongue sent my body soaring onto a wet cloud. Up against the wall he pushed me gingerly, and held my arms above my head.

"Tell me what you want me to do to you."
He whispered into my mouth. I licked my lips slowly as he watched. "You're already doing it." I answered.

In that moment with him, whatever nervousness or shyness I once had, was completely gone. And there weren't any wandering thoughts in my mind, or thoughts that weren't supposed to be there.

Comfortable in my own skin, my own wants, and my own needs... I felt sexy. I felt liberated. I felt in control.

I felt fucking free.

He lifted me up and carried me into his bedroom
where he laid me on the edge of his bed and kneeled
down in front of me. Slowly, he took off my heels and
then started a treasure trail of kisses up each of my
legs—and I thought that I was going to fucking pass
out from the rush of both heat and excitement that was
moving quickly through my body.
I wanted to watch him, so I leaned myself up a little bit,
but he stopped me. "No." He said as he got up and
kissed me gently on the mouth. "I want to make you
feel like you've never felt before. So lay down, close
your eyes, and let me make you feel things."

Well shit.
He for damn sure didn't have to tell me twice.

I layed my head back down, closed my eyes like he'd
asked me to and surrendered my body to him. Back on
his knees, he continued on his mission, teasing me with
his mouth all along my legs and when he got to my
thighs, I let out a soft whimper of pleasure. As he
placed his kisses, he took his time pushing my dress
higher and higher until he was able to see my core.
"Your pussy is fucking beautiful." He said seductively.
Already from day one, I loved the sound of his deep

voice. But hearing the husky tone of it while he was turned on...

Oh. My. God.

It was *evvveeerything*, and I let out a moan at the sound of it. He gave me a couple more light kisses in-between the very top of my thighs, and then parted my middle, exposing my clit, and went to work. Every flick of his tongue sent jolts of electricity through my whole body, and I tossed and turned and begged and pleaded and cursed, as I held onto the top of his head for dear life. I knew that I was soaking wet because I could hear my juices moving around as he lapped them up greedily. The louder my moans grew, the quicker he moved his tongue. And the quicker he moved his tongue, the more my body trembled—and out of nowhere—my orgasm came crashing down like I had never felt before.

As I came, he moaned and held my hips steady as he wasted no time drinking me like I was the fucking fountain of youth. I didn't even know that my body could do that. I had never came that hard, or that much, in my fucking life.

Fuck.

I pushed his head away from between my shaking legs, "Come here." I managed to whisper. He crawled his way up and once we were face to face, I grabbed the collar of his shirt—"I wanna taste my juices off your tongue." "Fuck you're sexy B." He told me before obeying my command. As we kissed, I caressed the back of his head and spread my legs wider so he could relax his waist in-between them. I could feel how hard he was through his jeans as he pushed against me...

he already he felt so fucking good.

"Wait." I said as I pulled my lips away from his. "Get up for a second." He obliged, and quickly I got up from the bed, tiptoed into the other room and dug through my clutch for a condom. When I got back, he was sitting upright on the edge of bed and smiled at me as he noticed it between my fingers. "Oh so this was planned huh?"

I winked, and then peeled my dress up over my head and threw it gently at him. "Since the moment I woke up this morning."

Nathan loved my body that night like it had never been loved before. He was gentle, passionate, rough, and selfless all at the same time—the perfect mix.

I wanted to make him feel as good as he was making me feel, so I made sure to make him cum... twice. Once using my mouth and once using my expert riding skills. When we were done—and both blissfully exhausted—we laid silently wrapped in each other's arms. I sighed and he kissed me on the forehead.

"You good?" He asked.

I smiled. "Oh, I'm fucking great."

"Nah, you're actually amazing B." He said. "You're an amazing woman and I knew that the very first night I laid eyes on you."

Now, I know that words can sometimes be 'just words' but, as a woman sometimes it just feels good to hear certain words from a man—you know? Especially when the last man you were with neglected so many parts of you and beat down your self-esteem. I had already built a lot of myself back up before Nathan, so it wasn't like his words were validating me or anything, but they were still nice to hear. It felt good to be praised by a man for a change, instead of being constantly put down. I lifted my head and kissed him softly on his mouth. "You've been beyond the perfect gentleman Nathan. Thank you for being you."

He squeezed me tighter, "You deserve nothing less B. Nothing less."

We laid there a little while longer, enjoying the feel of our naked bodies pressed together, until the dark of the sky started to make it's way to a pale blue. "I've gotta go handsome." I whispered. "I've got an early morning and plus... walking around in your clubbing outfit from the night before, and fucked up hair at 12 in the afternoon just isn't cute."

He chuckled. "Your hair is perfect."

I looked up at him and frowned. "Nathan... my hair is fucked up. Don't start lying to me now."
He rolled me onto my back and planted kisses all over my face and I giggled. "Lemme throw on some clothes and I'll take you home."

"No it's okay." I said. "I'll grab a cab. Get some rest I know you have a busy day ahead of you too."

"Seriously?" He asked.

"Seriously." I assured him.

"Grab my jeans and take some money for the cab."

"Nathan, you literally pay for everything—I think I can pay my own cab home."

I kissed him on the nose, then wiggled out from underneath him and went into the bathroom to try somewhat "freshen up". I took a look in the mirror and lawd... my hair and my makeup were a hot mess. "Ew" I said shaking my head.

I washed my face quickly and then finger combed my hair as much as I could. When I emerged, Nathan was dressed in some sweats and a beater waiting for me. "What are you doing?" I asked. "Damn B. Can I at least walk you downstairs and make sure you get in the cab safely?"

Man.. he was a good dude for real.

We headed downstairs and a cab was already waiting for me. I looked at him, curiously. "I called one for you while you were in the bathroom. I didn't want you waiting longer than you needed to."

Did I mention he was a good dude?

He opened the door for me and then kissed me. "You're beautiful." He said—and I blushed.

"Text me when you get home so I know you're safe."

I gave the cab driver my address, and as he pulled off, I dug through my clutch for my phone to text my girls in our group chat, and noticed a hundred dollar bill—that was not mine—folded between my phone and my lipstick.

I shook my head and smiled. "Fucking Nathan."

. . .

Later that day, you know my girls wanted all the details—
"Soooo... was it big?"
"Was it long?"
"Did he eat it?"
"Did he beat it?"
"Did he cook you breakfast?"
"Were YOU his breakfast?"

"TELL US EVERYTHING."

But all I said was "let's just say today my glow is brought to you in full... by the D *and* the T."

And let me tell y'all that glow was refreshed a good twice a week. *Lissteeeeennn...*

Once that seal was broken, Nathan and I couldn't keep our hands off of each other. Sometimes I would find myself being like "skip the date—let's go straight to your place. We can order food later."

It was dope. He was dope. Our energy together was dope. What we had was dope. And my life, in all departments, was just fucking dope.

That was until, one of us decided to want more...

I promised myself so many times that I was going to do what I felt was best for me, as opposed to what anyone else "thought" was best for me... and it was about time that I started keeping my promises.

♥

14

The Crimson Kiss

"Why do you always do this?" Nathan asked me as I was pulling on my jeans. I had them half way up over my ass and stopped wriggling.

"Do what?"

"This!" He said pointing at my jeans. "Why do you always rush out of here? Why don't you ever spend the night with me? It would be nice to wake up to you in the morning sometimes."

God, here we fucking go.

I took a deep breath and looked at him. Damn he was fine. Laying on the bed, no shirt, muscles just chillin out in the open—but holy fuck my life I wasn't trying to hear this speech of his, yet again.

I finished getting on my jeans and spoke softly.

"I already told you, I just have this thing where I like sleeping in my own bed."

"Okay, so instead of you always coming here, why don't I just come over to your place and then you can sleep and wake up in your *own* bed with me beside you?" He was working my muthafucking nerves but still, I kept the softness in my tone as I answered him—"We've been through this too. I don't let dudes in my house." I grabbed my red t-shirt off of his dresser, pulled it over my head and scanned the room with my eyes for my clutch.

Where the fuck did I put it?

"B, I'm not just 'any dude' though. I mean we've been kickin' it together for a good couple of months now. I think that qualifies me for an 'in your house' pass."

Why can't he just shut up? Why can he just lay there, be sexy and shut the hell up.

Technically, I truly understood him and where he was coming from. I mean here we were getting down on a regular basis and he still hadn't stepped one foot in my house yet, but here's what I still don't think he quite understood about me—I wasn't that type of girl.

To each their own, but my home was literally my sanctuary. It was my energy, my space, my everything. It was the only place I had in the world that didn't remind me of any man—if that makes sense.

I didn't have to wake up in the morning and look over at the other side of the bed and have flashbacks of someone laying in it, or sit at my kitchen table and be reminded of someone else sitting at the spot across from me.

Know what I mean?

I was protective of my house. It represented parts of me that had been lost for so many years—peace, stability, and happiness. It represented the woman I decided that I wanted to be, and it represented shit being done MY way and without limits or compromise—and that meant something to me.

That meant everything to me.

No man had ever been in there and I wanted to keep it that way. For how long? I didn't know. But I did know that I wasn't ready to let someone into that space yet, and no one was going to try to make me feel guilty about that.

"Yes we've been kicking it for a good minute now, and I don't want to come across as an asshole for saying this but, it still doesn't qualify you for a '*in my house*' pass." I told him honestly. "I'm not your woman. You're not my man. And I thought that we were both on the same page with that." The conversation was starting to make me feel claustrophobic, I didn't like it.

Clutch, clutch, where the fuck is my clutch?

"Well then why don't we change that status?" I stopped eye scanning the room and looked at him—"What?" The seriousness of his proposal was written all over his face. "I mean, I like you B. I like you a lot. Being around you makes me happy, seeing your name on my screen when you call makes my whole day you don't even know." He scooted down to the end of the bed where I was standing and took my hand.

Why? I thought to myself. *Why does he have to do this?*

"I want you B. I want all of you, the real way. I want you to be mine and only mine."

See, now normally *any* other woman in that moment would have been completely head over heels—and I was to a certain extent don't get me wrong—the words falling out of his perfect mouth were enough to make any woman melt right then and there. Plus, women were already constantly throwing themselves at him left right and center. Like my girl said way back in the beginning "Everyone wanted Nathan."

... Everyone but me.

I was loving what we had the way it was, and I just didn't want anything more than that.
But all of a sudden, there he was sitting at the edge of his king size bed, holding my damn hand, staring into my damn face talking about how he wanted a damn committed relationship. As I looked at him, a tiny part of me couldn't help but wonder if the only reason why he wanted me to be "his" was because I was the only one who actually *didn't* want to be his. Nathan was so used to women chasing him 24/7, that maybe because I didn't do all of that, it made him want me more?

"Look," I began. "I like you too, and you know that. But I told you from the very beginning that I didn't want to do the whole commitment thing right now. I like my freedom." He patted the bed indicating for me to sit beside him, and though I really wanted the conversation to be over with because I really didn't want to explain myself any further, out of respect for him, I sat. "B. I know you're scared of being hurt again, but I'm telling you, I'm not going to do that to you." The thing is, as sincere as he *may* have been, it didn't matter. I wasn't going to change my mind. He was staring at me so fucking intensely, I was getting uncomfortable and it was giving me anxiety. I also knew that at this point, the wonderful arrangement we had going was shot to shit because now this very conversation would start becoming even more repetitive and more intense—and I didn't have time for that. I put my hand on his cheek and smiled at him, "ugh... you're so yummy. Kiss me right now." I purred.

Without hesitation, he leaned in and submitted to my demand. He kissed me softly at first, making my body tingle and my breath start to shorten, and then pulled me closer and began kissing me deeper and harder. I straddled him and lifted my shirt up over my head and let it fall to the ground. I had already made up my mind that it would be the last time that I would be with him—so why not have farewell sex? Two orgasms later, I rested my head on his chest while he laid on his back smiling. He kissed the top of my forehead. "Just think about what I said okay?"

I already did. The answer is no.

"I will." I lied.

Ten minutes later, he fell into a deep sleep and I kissed his chest quietly, then slowly inched out of the bed. I tiptoed around the room as quietly as I could so I wouldn't wake him, as I gathered my belongings and went into the bathroom to freshen up a bit and get dressed. When I came out, he was still asleep. I grabbed a pen and a pack of matches out of my clutch, ripped the back piece off of the matches and quickly scribbled—

"I had to go. Be good handsome. xxox."

I left the note on top of his phone so I knew he would see it when he woke, and tiptoed my way out of his house with my heels in my hand.

I was a good girl who had a bad habit of putting other people's wants and needs above my own. I'm still a good girl though... it's just that now I have a good habit of using the word "no" whenever I need to, and not feeling the slightest bit guilty about it.

♥

15

True To Myself

About a month had passed since I ended things with
Nathan. Of course he had called me the next morning
after I had left him fast asleep in his bliss, and he wasn't
happy about what I had to say, but he had no choice
but to accept it. Maybe other people who were on the
outside looking in, would tell me that I'm fucked up,
or that I'm crazy. Maybe they would even be upset at
the fact that I would "let such a good man go" but
here's the thing—when men aren't ready to be the men
for us that we need, don't we say shit like "so let us go
instead of dragging us along."? Well, it was the same
shit here just genders reversed. He wanted more from
me than I was ready to give—I wasn't ready to be
someone's woman—and I wasn't about to play with
his emotions because _that's_ not right.

It was great while it lasted, and I would for sure miss
him, but this was me staying true to myself without
purposely hurting anyone else in the process...
And I wasn't sorry for that.

Sometimes, simply ignoring the Devil doesn't work. Sometimes, you have to kick his ass right back down to fucking hell where he belongs.

♥

16

Drug Addict

I was leaving work and I'd had the worst day ever.

I was tired, my feet hurt, I had a pounding headache and to top it all off my period had come two days early and the cramps were kicking my ass. All I wanted to do was go home, bathe, drink a bottle of wine, and watch re-runs of The Fresh Prince Of Bel-Air in my bed until I passed out.

I was replying to my group chat as I walked across the parking lot, and when I got to my car, I looked up and instantly my headache went from pounding, to nails on a chalkboard. "Jesus fuck—no." I said to my ex who had the audacity to be leaned up against my car waiting for me. He held up his hands defensively, "Wait, don't trip on me please. I promise I come in peace."

This is not happening right now man.

"I don't care if you came dipped in 24 karat gold and coated in 600 princess cut diamonds you fucking idiot, GET OFF OF MY CAR, AND AWAAAY FROM ME."

Was he for real?

"Okay, I deserved that and I knew you weren't going to be thrilled to see me here, but if you could just wait a minute and hear me out, I just wan..." —

"Bro, holy fuck, NOO." I snapped, cutting him off. "No I cannot wait a minute and hear you out. How many fucking minutes of my life have I already wasted on hearing *you* out? Now you want me to give you *more* minutes? You just have to have more of MY life minutes to fucking waste now don't you, because God forbid it would ever cross your selfish little brain to STOP wasting my life minutes!"

I closed my eyes and rubbed my forehead with my free hand, all while trying to force the huge lump that was forming in my throat back down.

Don't cry B. Don't let this idiot see you cry again.

"Can you move from my car please?" I asked, eyes still closed. "I am going to move from your car, I promise, I didn't track you down to start trouble. I just couldn't stop thinking about you. That night I saw you at the club you looked so good, so perfect, and I followed you outside because I wanted you to know that I've never stopped loving you—ever. Seeing you made me realize how badly I fucked up, but before I got the chance to tell you all of that, you flipped out and then your girl came outside and double flipped out and I.. well... I reacted like a jerk. And I wanted you to know that I'm sorry."

You know what this was right? This was him thinking that I was still the same old B. He thought that I still loved him. He thought that I was going to calm down, let him take me in his arms while I cried, while he would then tell me all of the things that I *used* to want to hear from his mouth.
Well surprise fucking surprise bitch. The old B moved out a while ago and is never coming back.

Behold the *new* B.

I opened my eyes and stared directly at him. "You're not sorry. You're searching for an ego boost, and you probably haven't found anyone who gave it to you quite like I used to. You're sick. You're a really sick man. Don't you get it? You cut my soul more times than you ever kissed it, and broke my spirit more times than you ever lifted it. You took more good from me than you ever gave back to me, and you stood there and watched me bawl my eyes out more than you ever comforted me. You watered my insecurities with pleasure, helping them to grow stronger, and shushed my voice and my expressions so that I could remain, in your eyes, smaller than you. You used my weaknesses against me, threw my past back in my face and I stayed. Time after time I stayed, and that—me staying—boosted your ego. So now you see me, flying higher than you would have ever *allowed* me to, and it makes you sick. You've become sick because *I* was your drug. *I* was what kept you going.

Breaking me down was what made you feel powerful. Strong. Dominant... and now look at you..." I waved a lazy finger at him and shook my head. "Sick, pale and out of power. I stopped giving you your drug. No more ego boosts for you. And I'm glad you haven't come across another woman who will give it to you either. Now, I'm going to ask you one last time, to move from my vehicle before I call the police, get you thrown in jail for the weekend for stalking and harassment, and slap you with a pretty restraining order."

He stood there, half confused and half angry. "You would seriously go as far as to call the police on me?" I held up my phone and punched in the numbers 9-1-1.

"Please, try me." I said. He nodded his head and slowly, took a couple of steps away from my car.

"You aren't the same girl you used to be."

I unlocked my doors with my remote and pushed passed him. "Nope. I sure the fuck ain't and thank the good Lord." I said as I climbed inside my car, slammed the door shut, and hit that gas pedal as hard as I could.

At the end of the day—no matter where we come from, what we do for a living, how we look, or how we were raised—we all know what it feels like to have had our hearts broken. We're women.

♥

17

Hennessy And Heartbeats

Jazzy, Erika, Angel and I sat around my rooftop pool in our bathing suits, with our feet in the water. "How you feeling B?" Angel asked lighting a cigarette. I splashed the water a little with my feet and looked out into the city. "I'm alright." I answered dryly. "Are you alright as in, you're really alright, or are you '_I'm saying I'm alright, but I'm lying_' type of alright?" Jazzy asked. I winced and shrugged my shoulders. "It's hard to explain" I started. "Like, I was so mad last night y'all. Like so fucking mad. And then I was mad at myself for even allowing him to make me mad like that _again_. You know?" My girls nodded their heads, understanding.

"I shouldn't have even said anything to him. I should have turned around and went back inside work, or called the police right away and let them deal with him, but... I unno. I just couldn't ignore his sense of entitlement. He's like a fucking blood sucker I swear to God he is. He's so disgusting... makes me fucking sick to my stomach. This is exactly why I call him a monster

or the Devil—because of this shit. After all this time
has passed, I would have liked to hope that he had
changed. Like sincerely though."

I took a cigarette from Angels pack and lit it. I don't
think anyone really knew what to say in the moment,
so we all just kind of stayed quiet. "Am I traumatized?"
I suddenly asked my girls. "Is this why I got so mad last
night, and the time before?" Jazzy handed me her glass
of Hennessy and I took a sip.

"Maybe you are traumatized. And maybe that's not the
end of the world." she said. "The shit you went
through with him was real life. It broke you. It
degraded you. You had to build yourself back up again
from fucking scratch—and that ain't easy. People make
light of shit like that, and it's nothing light at all. It's
like a drunk driver crashing his car into yours and you
surviving, but your legs are fucked up, and all the
doctors say that you should have been dead and that
you must have had a bunch of angels with you.
Even though you survived, have done your therapy for
years, got the movement back in your legs and can walk
perfectly normal again—you still have those visible
scars left on them. And every time you bathe, or wear
shorts or a skirt and look at those scars, you're

reminded of that piece of shit drunk driver that almost took your life that night.

Fuckboy, is that piece of shit drunk driver. So while yes, you're going through life doing more than fine, every time he shows up it brings you back—his face is your scar. And yes, as much as you've taken responsibility for not leaving him when you should have, the fact still remains that he ripped your fucking heart out man. He hurt you badly, and on purpose, so it's like... you have every right to feel what you feel when he pops up like a fucking idiot. You could have came out of that heartbreak as a seriously bitter and ruined woman. You could have been one of those women who just walks through life holding onto that shit *fooooreevvver* and taking it out on random people who had nothing to do with anything—but you didn't. You did your part and healed yourself. But just because you're healed, doesn't mean you aren't allowed to have moments. You're too hard on yourself B. Chill. Just because you're a strong woman, doesn't mean that you aren't allowed to have moments of weakness. You're allowed."

Jazzy words really hit home, and once again, I started to cry and all of my girls moved in closer to me for a group hug. She was right—I was allowed to have my moments.

After about two minutes of hugging, Angel broke the silence. "It's true what Jazz said—things could be way worse. You could have ended up one of them bitter bitches who comments retarded and rude shit under people's youtubes. Think about how pitiful someone's life has to be to end up at *that* point."

"Only you would come with some shit like that to say." Erika said, and we all started laughing. "I love y'all man." I said breaking free from the hugs and wiping my face. "I really do."

"We got your back B." Erika said. "Always have and always will." Jazzy added.

"Alright enough of all this mushy shit. Y'all know B will cry all damn day if you let her with her Pisces self." Angel said. She grabbed the bottle of Hennessy and stood up—"SHOTS!" She yelled. "Shots and then we goin' out tonight because it's fucking Saturday, and fuck it... we celebrating LIFE, all of the good things life is going to bring us, and sista-hood. Let's go paint the town B's favorite color—*crimson*." She winked at me and I smiled.

"Alright well let's at least order some food right quick before Angel gets shot happy, and gets us all fucked right up. I think pizza is the best bet right now." Erika said grabbing my phone since it was the closest. She typed in my password—"Oh hold up, you got a text."

"Who's it from?" I asked.

"Nathan." She answered giving me a side eye and a sly smirk.

"Since when y'all started talking again?" Jazzy asked. "I mean I guess since right now. We haven't spoken since I ended things." I took my phone from Erika, opened his message, and was immediately caught off guard by the length of it as I scanned it quickly.

"Now you know you need to read that out loud." Angel said lighting another cigarette. "Don't be leaving us in the dark now."

I cleared my throat and began to read.

"Good afternoon pretty lady. I know this message might be random but you've been on my mind this past week, heavy, and I just wanted to tell you a couple of things. For starters, I want you to know that you're beautiful—inside and outside. I have never met a woman quite like you. You're charming, incredibly

independent, polite, open but reserved and mysterious at the same time. You were a breath of fresh air for me, and I never said thank you before, so I'm saying it now... thank you. As much as I wanted you to be mine alone, and was kind of hurt in a way that things had to end, I was also really proud of you. Proud because you stood firm in what you wanted, and what would be best for you at the time. As weird as this may sound, I grew an entire new level of respect for you because of that.

I hope you stay that way, and you continue to stand firmly in yourself, and that you don't settle for anything in life—and I do mean anything.

I know that you've been through so much already, but know that you are extremely blessed by the man above as he has provided you with an abundance of courage, will, and determination—and with those three things alone you will conquer any obstacle that comes your way. You are also surrounded by women who love and look out for you. Your girls are solid. Trust me I've been around many women in my life, and the foundation and morals of your squad is damn near extinct in these streets. They too are a blessing... You are all blessed to have each other. You're a special woman B, and I hope that you'll remind yourself of *that every day—don't ever let any nigga out here ever make you feel otherwise. You're a lady, you're a Queen and you deserve to be treated as such, always. Take care of yourself. And if you ever need me for anything at all, no matter the time... I got you."*

Erika, Angel and Jazzy stood speechless in front of me. I looked up at them, placed a hand over my heart...

and blushed.

Epilogue

Nathan was very right about me having been through a lot of shit already, and the heartbreaks along the way are only the half of it. I haven't always done the right things, nor have I always kept all of the promises that I've made to myself along the way but, you know what? Every step that I've ever taken, and every corner that I've ever turned, lead me to exactly where I was supposed to be. Funny how we only see that looking backwards, isn't it?

This was my story, but it's dedicated to every woman who reads it. I hope that if you take away anything from this book, it would be these two things:

1. Taking a time-out from being someone else's woman, to learn how to be your own woman first, is probably one of the most important and best things that you could ever do for yourself.

And 2. Our girlfriends need more credit than we give them, because often, they are the ones holding us up and keeping us sane, when we feel like we're going to break down and lose our minds.

I don't know what I would have done without the women who have been there for me when I needed them, and have been there for me... just because.

Sending much love to all of you Queens out there.

Now go call your bestie's and tell them that you love them.

Xxox,

Cici. B

Acknowledgments

Mom, if it weren't for you encouraging me to write...
I have no idea where I would be right now, or how I
would be able to deal with this thing called life. Thank
you for picking up on my extreme shyness and anxiety
when it came to voicing what was on my mind, and
putting a pen in my hand to help me deal with it at
such an early age. You are, and have always been, my
best friend. You've never judged me for any situation I
have ever been in, or put myself in, and I don't know if
you'll ever really understand just how much that has
meant to me. Thank for being my shoulder to cry on,
my person to laugh with, my backbone to help my
stand tall, and my motivational speaker—even in times
when you were down and weren't feeling good.

Watching you fight for everything my brothers and I
had my entire life, taught me to never be a quitter.
Watching you work two-three jobs, come home
exhausted, yet still manage to make dinner, help us
with homework, bathe us and get us ready for
bed—taught me how to go hard in anything I started
in my own life, and to get shit done without excuses.

You were always my idol, and you still are.

I may not have always made the right choices in my life
and I've taken *a lot* of wrong turns (and have done a lot
of stupid shit lol) but you've always taught me that it's

okay to make mistakes as long as I learn from them, and so here I am...

I've learned, and I keep learning, every day.

You have to know that you aren't just my rock mom—you're my whole entire heart.

Luv you mommy.

Blush

Cici. B

Twitter-Facebook-Instagram @TheCrimsonKiss

Made in the USA
San Bernardino, CA
07 November 2016